POCKET GUIDE TO

Speed Records

ANDREW DUNCAN

POCKET GUIDE TO
Speed Records

ANDREW DUNCAN

CRESCENT BOOKS
New York • Avenel, New Jersey

©1993 Salamander Books Ltd.,
129-137 York Way,
London N7 9LG,
United Kingdom.

This 1993 edition published by Crescent Books,
distributed by Outlet Book Company, Inc.,
a Random House Company, 40 Engelhard Avenue,
Avenel, New Jersey 07001

ISBN 0-517-08656-5

8 7 6 5 4 3 2 1

Credits
Editor: Tony Hall
Designer: Paul Johnson
Picture research: Tony Moore
Filmset: The Old Mill, London

Color reproduction: P&W Graphics PTE Ltd, Singapore
Printed in Belgium by Proost International Book Production

Picture credits
Cover: Salamander Books; Endpapers: Quadrant; Half-
title, Title: Salamander Books; Pg 5, 6: Salamander
Books; Pgs 7, 8: Quadrant; Pgs 10, 11, 12, 13: Quadrant;
Pg 14: Don Morley; Pg 15: Jaguar; Pgs 16, 17, 19:
Salamander Books; Pgs 20, 21, 22, 23, 24: Don Morley;
Pg 25, 26, 27: Quadrant; Pg 28: Salamander Books; Pg
30: Ajax Features; Pgs 31, 32, 33: Salamander Books;
Vosper MTB, Ajax Features; Pgs 34, 35, 36, 37, 38, 39:
Ajax Features; *Elf Aquitaine*, Jonathan Eastland; Pgs 40,
41, 42, 43, 44, 45, 46, 47, 48, 49, 50, 51, 52, 53:
Salamander Books; Pg 54: Quadrant; Pg 55: Salamander
Books; Pg 56: Rex Features; Pg 57, 58, 59, 60, 61, 62,
63: Salamander Books.

Author
Andrew Duncan is a professional writer and historian,
based in London. He writes on the history of the city,
and on many other subjects, including technology and
engineering.

Contents

Introduction

Thanks to technology, the speed at which vehicles travel and machines operate has reached a level which would have boggled the imagination of people living only a century ago.

Then, a relatively slow train or a turbine-powered ship would have been the nearest anyone got to the sensation — the thrill even — of high speed.

Today we all drive around in cars capable of well over 160.9km/h (100mph). And jet flight has made travel at hundreds of miles an hour, if not an everyday experience, then certainly an unexceptional one for millions of people.

Meanwhile, operating at the furthest limits of technology, inspired amateurs in search of world records and calculating technicians obeying political, military or scientific imperatives continue to raise the absolute speed stakes higher and higher.

No-one can say where it will all end. All we can be certain of is that a century from now our children will be traveling a good deal faster than we are today — especially in the air, where everyday hypersonic flight in and out of the atmosphere is already virtually a reality.

Speed Records surveys the exciting world of speed as it is today, and celebrates the fastest in all significant areas of technology: on land, cars of all descriptions, motorcycles, and trains; on water, everything from sailboards to yachts to powerboats; in the air, propeller and jet aircraft and spaceships; and finally, in a special short section, weapons from arrows to ICBMs, and machines such as computers and printers. The main sections are all prefaced by brief histories of the land, water, and air speed records.

We guarantee you lots of thrills and plenty of surprises — and above all a better understanding of speed and where the pursuit of this thrilling but elusive commodity is taking us.

Below: *A British Rail diesel HST 125 locomotive. Two of these broke the diesel train speed record in 1987.*

Left: *The Bell X-2 research craft after its first flight on 18 November 1955. X-2 broke Mach 3 on 23 July 1956.*

Section One: Land

The Story of the Land Speed Record (LSR)

The story of the LSR goes back to December 1898, when the Comte de Chasseloup-Laubat using automotive power clocked 63.15km/h (39.24mph) over a one-way kilometre at Agricole Park near Paris. His achievement, remarkable for its time, sparked off a tussle with his great Belgian rival Camille Jenatzy, a tussle which produced five new records in as many months culminating in Jenatzy's 105.9km/h (65.79mph) in April 1899.

These two pioneers of speed drove electric cars. Steam cars also played their part in the early days, one of the famous Stanley Steamers producing a new record of 195.65km/h (121.57mph) in 1906.

From that time on petrol-engined cars were to dominate the scene.

Great strides were made in the '20s and '30s, when two Englishmen, Sir Malcolm Campbell and Sir Henry Segrave, fought for the title of fastest man on wheels.

Campbell topped 241km/h (150mph) in Wales in 1925. Driving on Daytona Beach, Florida, Segrave became the first man to break the 322km/h (200mph) barrier. His 1,000hp Sunbeam was the first specially designed LSR car.

Segrave's early death in 1930 left the field clear for Campbell and his famous *Bluebird*s. By 1935 Campbell had broken

Left: The official Land Speed Record-holding car of 1983. Briton Richard Noble's jet-powered Thrust 2.

the official LSR nine times and raised it to over 482.7km/h (300mph). To this day he remains the most successful LSR breaker of all time.

Another Englishman, John Cobb, took the record up to over 563km/h (350mph) before World War II. After the war (1947) he raised it still further to — 634km/h (394mph).

That record lasted for 15 years and was only beaten after Malcolm Campbell's son Donald had spent nine years and £2 million ($4 million) ironing out problems with his gas turbine, aero-engined *Bluebird*.

The day of the wheel-driven LSR car was over, however. Even before *Bluebird* had topped 643.7km/h (400mph) in 1964, Craig Breedlove's jet-powered *Spirit of America* had become the fastest car on earth. And when jet and rocket cars were recognized by the LSR governing body, the way was open for them to become the official world LSR holders.

Having broken the 804km/h (500mph) barrier in the heady year of 1964, during which the LSR was broken six times, Breedlove went on to crack 956.6km/h (600mph) in 1965. That record stood for five years. Today, almost 30 years on, the official LSR is still only some 53.1km/h (33mph) higher.

Speed Records on Land

The highest speed at which any vehicle has ever traveled across the earth's surface is 4,972km/h (3,090mph). This was the peak velocity of a rocket-propelled sled riding on railed tracks at Holloman Air Force Base, near Albuquerque, New

Mexico, on 19 February 1959. No humans were on board at the time, though the sled had carried passengers on earlier trips, even up to supersonic speeds. The runs were made as part of research carried out by the US Air Force into, amongst other things, the problems of escaping from high-speed aircraft.

We have a section later on rail speed records, but in the meantime we begin our survey of land speed records with a look at cars built specially to achieve the world land speed record. Inevitably, these are generally the fastest machines on the surface of the earth.

World Land Speed (LSR) Record-Attempting Cars

Currently the *official* record-holder is British driver Richard Noble. On 4 October 1983 he drove his jet-powered, solid aluminum-wheeled *Thrust 2* twice over a measured mile distance of the Black Rock Desert, Nevada, USA, to average 1,019.467km/h (633.468mph). His peak speed, achieved during the second run, was 1,046km/h (650mph). For Noble, a salesman from Twickenham, Middlesex, winning the record was the fulfillment of a nine-year dream (as well as the termination of 19 years of US dominance of the LSR). Development of the car began with only £150 ($300), the scrap value of the wrecked *Thrust 1*. The engine, a 7,711kg (17,000 lb) thrust Rolls-Royce Avon 302 turbojet from an F-6 Lightning fighter plane, was bought from the RAF for a special concessionary price.

Unofficially, the fastest unguided vehicle on land, and the fastest rocket-engined car, is the *Budweiser Rocket*, a blisteringly fast three-wheeler which was driven at 1,190.377km/h (739.666mph or Mach 1.0106) by Stan Barrett of the USA at

Above: Blue Flame, *the world's fastest rocket-engined car, traveled at 1,001.4km/h (622.2mph) in October 1970.*

Edwards Air Force Base in California on 17 December 1979. Unfortunately, Barrett, a former US Air Force pilot and a well-known film stuntman, could not claim the official Fédération Internationale d'Automobile (FIA) record because his car could not hold enough fuel for the requisite one-mile run; nor could it be refueled within the one-hour gap allowed between qualifying runs. However, the speed is almost certainly correct because it was monitored both by the Air Force and by sophisticated telemetry equipment on board the *Rocket* itself, which relayed essential data from the car while it was in motion back to a mobile computer command post.

The *Rocket* was powered by a 48,000hp Romatec V4 rocket engine and a US Navy Sidewinder missile. The Sidewinder, adding a further 12,900hp, cut in when Barrett pressed a special button on the steering wheel at 984km/h (612mph).

As well as becoming the fastest man on earth, Barrett also became the first man to exceed the speed of sound on land. His car, traveling faster than a bullet and reaching a speed of 644km/h (400mph) in just 3 seconds, literally outran the roar of its own engine.

Officially, the world's fastest *rocket-engined* car is Gary Gabelich's *Blue Flame*. Way back in October 1970 this topped the 1,000km/h (621.4mph) mark by traveling at 1,001.473km/h (622.287mph) on the Bonneville Salt Flats in Utah, USA. The 11.6 metre (38ft)-long *Blue Flame*, powered by hydrogen peroxide and liquid natural gas, held the world land speed record for 9 years. Sadly, Gabelich, a former NASA trainee astronaut and drag-racer, was killed in a motorcycle accident in 1984 close to his Long Beach, California, home. An ironic way to go for a man who had cheated death at phenomenal speeds for so long.

Two more car speed records were set even earlier than Gabelich's.

In July 1964 Donald Campbell of the UK, in a very brave run on a bad course, set the record for a wheel-driven car on the salt waste of Lake Eyre in Australia, when *Bluebird* hit 690.909km/h (429.311mph) at the fastest section of the

Right: *Donald Campbell's record-breaking car* Bluebird. *In 1964 in Australia this vehicle hit 690.9km/h (429.3mph).*

measured distance (he also set a new LSR, but it only lasted a few months). 'Wheel-driven' means that the power which drives the vehicle is transmitted directly from the engine *through* the wheels, rather than by jet or rocket thrust.

And a little over a year later, in November 1965, Bob Summers of the USA set the record for a *piston-engined* wheel-driven car (*Bluebird* had a turbine aero engine) when he drove his beautiful *Goldenrod* at 673.516km/h (418.504mph) on the Bonneville Salt Flats.

Actually Summers set the record for a multi-piston-engined car because *Goldenrod*, although only 0.7 metres (28in) high (excluding the tailfin), packed in no fewer than four Chrysler V8 engines, set in line with the driver at the rear. The single piston-engined speed record was set when Al Teague, also of the USA, drove his *Speed O Motive* at 640.446km/h (397.996mph) on the Bonneville Flats 15 years later, in November 1989.

To purists, although free-wheeling jet and rocket cars have gone much faster, *Goldenrod* remains the real land speed record champion because it was both piston-engined and wheel-driven just like any conventional car. As if in testimony to that fact, the car now tours the world pulling in huge crowds at car shows and exhibitions.

The next challenge to the land speed record may well come from veteran of the scene Craig Breedlove, the Californian hot rodder who broke the record way back in 1963 with *Spirit of America*, the first jet-powered car. Although he later lost the record, he won it back on several occasions, the last being in 1965 when he broke the 966.54km/h (600mph) barrier with *Sonic I*, powered by a General Electric J79 jet engine (as used in the F-104 fighter plane). Breedlove has recently acquired another *two* J79s for his latest project, so watch this space!

Below: *Seen on the Bonneville Salt Flats in 1965, the enormous multi-engined* Goldenrod, *driven by Bob Summers.*

Drag Racers

After these highly-specialized LSR machines, the fastest cars are drag racers, both piston-engined and thrust-powered. Their general objective is to accelerate as fast as possible and to cover the 402.34 metres (quarter mile) from a standing start in the shortest possible time. Lowest elapsed time (LET) is the time taken to cover this distance. Highest terminal velocity (HTV) is the highest speed at the end of the run. Obviously the dragster with the fastest acceleration will have the lowest LET, although not necessarily the highest HTV.

Above: *Craig Breedlove in action driving the record-breaking first jet-powered car,* Spirit of America.

Sammy Miller of the USA set the LET record in 1986 when his Pontiac 'Funny Car' took just 3.58 seconds to cover the standing quarter mile (402.34 metres).

The current HTV record for any drag racer is 631.732km/h (392.54mph), set by Kitty Hambleton of the USA at El Mirage Dry Lake, California, on 7 July 1977.

For piston-engined dragsters, the LET record for the stand-

Above: *The fastest on the Grand Prix circuit, Briton Nigel Mansell driving a Williams-Honda car in 1987.*

ing quarter mile (402.34 metres) was set by Joe Amato at Gainesville, Florida, in March 1991. The HTV record is 476.43km/h (296.05mph), set by Gary Ormsby of the USA at Topeka, Kansas, in September 1990.

Racing Cars

With racing cars, the next fastest after dragsters, lap speeds and race times are naturally more important measurements than absolute speed. It's not necessarily the fastest car that wins the race.

In the motor-racing world there are two types of circuit: closed and road. Closed are faster than road.

The record for the highest average lap speed on a closed circuit is 403.878km/h (250.958mph). This was achieved by Dr Hans Liebold of Germany driving a turbocharged experimental Mercedes coupé on the Nardo track in Italy on 5 May 1979.

Frenchman Henri Pescarolo holds the same record for a road circuit. Driving a Matra Simca sports car at Francorchamps near Spa, Belgium, on 6 May 1973, he averaged 262.461km/h (163.086mph) over the 14.10km (8.76 mile) circuit.

Nigel Mansell of the UK holds the record for the fastest average speed on a Grand Prix circuit in current use. Driving a Williams-Honda in the Austrian Grand Prix at Zeltweg on 16 August 1987, he turned in consistently high lap speeds to produce a world-beating average of 235.421km/h (146.284mph) for the race.

In the fastest race in the world, the Busch Clash at Daytona, Florida, USA, the cars race much faster than Grand Prix cars. The record average speed to date for the 80.5km (50mile) race is 318.322km/h (197.802mph), achieved by Bill Elliott in 1987 driving a Ford Thunderbird.

At Le Mans the record average speed for the 24-hour race (during which the fastest cars cover well over 4,800km (3,000 miles) is 221.63km/h (137.718mph). And at Indianapolis, an 804km (500 mile) race which takes less than 3 hours, it is 299.299km/h (185.891mph). The cars involved were, respectively, a Jaguar XJR-9 and a Lola-Chevrolet.

Road Vehicles
Off the race-track and on the road, the fastest road car at the moment is the Koenig Porsche C62, Willy Koenig's version of the Le Mans-winning 956/962 sports racing car. It has a 3.2-liter twin turbo engine, and is capable of 0-62mph in 3.5 seconds and a top speed of 146km/h (236mph). Only 30 are to be made, little modified from the original apart from a more user-friendly gearbox. Several have already been delivered — at a cost of £800,000 ($1.5 million) each!

In the not too distant future, the Koenig Porsche will be upstaged by the JaguarSport XJR-15, a 6-liter car costing £561,000 ($1 million) and capable of 153.3km/h (274mph). Fifty will be built as part of a one-make race series. After that, owners will be able to take the cars — re-bodied versions of the 1988 Le Mans-winning XJR-9 — on the road with little modification except for such legal necessities as bumpers, doors, locks, indicators, and rear view mirrors.

Below: *Racing to be faster than the Porsche C62 is the 146km/h-236mph) JaguarSport XJR-15.*

The fastest *production* car ever built is the Jaguar XJ220, a £415,000 ($690,000) supercar now being assembled in a limited edition of 350 at Bloxham, Oxfordshire, in England. In July 1992 British racing driver Martin Brundle drove the car on the Nardo banked circuit in southern Italy at 349.21km/h (217.1mph), the equivalent of 358.86km/h (223.6mph) on the open road. Admittedly the car's catalytic convertors had been taken off to increase its brake horsepower for the record-breaking run, thus rendering it immediately non-standard and

Below: *Following a test drive in 1992, Jaguar's limited edition XJ220 became the world's fastest production car.*

Above: *The Ferrari F40 supercar. The production car with the fastest recorded acceleration in the world.*

therefore non-production, but until another close challenger comes along, the point seems academic. The famous Italian automobile manufacturer Bugatti is reported as being in the wings with a challenger.

To date, the production car with the most rapid recorded acceleration is the Ferrari F40. Two drivers from *Fast Lane* magazine took one from 0-96.55km/h (0-60mph) in just 3.98 seconds at Millbrook, England, on 9 February 1989.

Diesel-powered cars are generally slower than those with petrol engines, but they can still be surprisingly swift. The fastest diesel car on record is the prototype 3-liter Mercedes C111/3. In October 1978 it reached a speed of 327.3km/h (203.3mph) during tests on the Nardo circuit in Italy.

Solar and Other Unusually Powered Machines

Experimental or novelty cars whose power is derived from non-oil-based fuels can also manage to achieve quite respectable speeds.

The quickest steam car, for example, is *Steamin' Demon*. Built by the Barber-Nichols Engineering Company and driven by Robert Barber on the famous Bonneville Salt Flats, it has literally steamed along at speeds up to a recorded maximum of 234.33km/h (145.607mph). The story goes, however, that Fred Marriott went slightly faster than that way back in January 1907 while driving one of the famous Stanley Steamers called Wogglebug on Daytona Beach. Unfortunately during the run he hit a sand ridge and overturned during his historic run so his claimed speed of 241.3km/h (150mph) cannot be officially verified.

On 25 June 1990 Christopher Sleath of Market Harborough, England, clinched the world land speed record for an electric car over 1 km with a flying start when he drove his vehicle at 100.06km/h (62.18mph).

Considerably slower but nevertheless remarkable is *Sunraycer*, the world's fastest solar-powered vehicle. Manufactured by General Motors, this ultimate in 'green machines' achieved 78.37km/h (48.71mph) at Mesa, Arizona, on 24 June 1988.

Combining solar and electric power produces much better results. Star Micronics' solar-cum-battery-powered car *Solarstar* was driven at a world record speed of 134.98km/h (83.88mph) at Richmond RAAF base, Australia, on 5 January 1991.

Even the wind has been harnessed in man's pursuit of speed. John Buckstaff holds the official ice-yachting speed

Right: *Even tanks can boast the power of Jaguar engines. Here the British Scorpion AFV races into action.*

record. As long ago as 1938, he traveled at 230km/h (143mph) on Lake Winnebago, Wisconsin, USA. Here surely is a record waiting to be broken! (Be it noted, however, that Buckstaff's is not the absolute ice speed record. That accolade goes to Sammy Miller, who drove his *rocket*-powered sled on Lake George, New York, on 15 February 1981 at 399km/h (247.93mph)).

The *official* speed record for yachting on dry land belongs to Frenchman Christian-Yves Nau. He set it on 22 March 1981 when he hit 107km/h (66.48mph) at Le Touquet in France. *Unofficially* the record belongs to American Nord Embroden, who is said to have achieved 142.26km/h (88.4mph) at Superior Dry Lake, California, USA, in April 1976.

In all high-speed, hard-surface yachting, the wind has to be exceptionally strong. In both the official record-achieving runs noted above, the wind was blowing at over 112.6km/h (70mph).

Big Machines

Some big, heavy machines designed for purposes other than speed can go surprisingly fast.

The world's fastest tank, for example, is the British Scorpion AFV (Armored Fighting Vehicle). Although weighing in at 8,073kg (17,800.965lb-7.94 tons) when prepared for combat, it is still capable of 80.5km/h (50mph), thanks to its 4.2 liter militarized Jaguar engine.

And if your house is unfortunate enough to go up in flames, hope your local fire station has a fleet of Chubb Firefighters

at its disposal. One of these cumbersome machines achieved an incredible 210.13km/h (130.57mph) when servicing Richard Noble's *Thrust 2* (see above, p10) during land speed record trials in the United States. Like the Scorpion tank and several other record-breaking vehicles, the Chubb packs a Jaguar engine under its hood.

Motorcycles

Driving at high speed cocooned inside a big, stable machine planted firmly on the ground is one thing. But to do it perched on two wheels surely requires an extra level of nerve. Yet motorcycles have been ridden at speeds in excess of 482.7km/h (300mph).

There is nice symmetry in the fact that the world speed record for a two-wheeled machine is almost exactly half that for a four-wheeler.

The record is 512.733km/h (318.598mph); it was achieved by US Yamaha dealer Donald Vesco riding a 6.3 metres (21ft)-long double Kawasaki-engined machine named *Lightning Bolt* on Bonneville Salt Flats in August 1978. On his fastest run he actually achieved an average a little higher than that: 513.165km/h (318.865mph). The speed was less than the 523km/h (325mph) at which he had been aiming, but as well as winning him the motorcycle speed record it also made him the first man to exceed 500km/h (310.7mph) on two wheels. Streamlined and powered by methane, *Lightning Bolt* was so fast that it had to have parachutes as well as brakes to help slow it down.

For sheer acceleration, aspiring speedsters have yet to beat Henk Vink of the Netherlands and Bo O'Brechta of the USA. It was back in 1980 that the latter, riding a supercharged 1,200cc Kawasaki, rocketed from a standing start to the quarter-mile marker (402.34 metres) in just 7.8 seconds. And it was even longer ago than that — 24 July 1977 to be precise — that Henk Vink, also riding a Kawasaki, covered 1km (0.6214

Above: *Record-breaking rider Donald Vesco, who rode the double Kawasaki-engined* Lightning Bolt *in August 1978.*

Right: *Canadian rider Yvon du Hamel produced the world's highest average lap speed at Daytona Speedway in 1973.*

miles) from a standing start in just 16.68 seconds. Vink made two runs over a measured distance within a fixed time limit, which meant that his achievement qualified as an official world record.

Motorcycle Racing

On the race track, motorcycles are not quite as fast as cars. Riding on the Daytona International Speedway in Florida, USA, in March 1973 Yvon du Hamel of Canada set the record for the highest average lap speed for a closed circuit when he attained 257.958km/h (160.288mph).

The fastest road circuit is Dundrod in Co. Antrim, Northern Ireland, where the Ulster Grand Prix is held. In August 1990 Steve Hislop of Scotland won the circuit this prized trophy when he averaged 195.5km/h (121.46mph) over the course during the King of the Road race. (On the same occasion he also set a lap record of 199.10km/h (123.72mph)).

Only tenths of a second slower than Dundrod is the circuit of the Isle of Man TT, the oldest established motorcycle race in the world. Here the record average race speed is 194.87km/h (121.09mph). Once again it was set by Scottish rider Steve Hislop, this time riding in 1991. He also holds the circuit lap record of 198.72km/h (123.48mph).

The best known annual motorcycle race in the US is the Daytona 200, a 321.87km (200-mile) contest over 57 laps of the Daytona International Speedway, Daytona Beach, Florida. The lap record, set by Tom Stevens on a Yamaha in 1990, is 180.04km/h (111.87mph). The highest average speed for

Left: Steve Hislop on the Isle of Man TT circuit, during his record-breaking ride in 1991.

Above: *The motorcycle with a fair claim to be the fastest production machine is the Kawasaki Tu Atara YB6 E1.*

the race, achieved by Kenny Roberts, also on a Yamaha, in 1984, is 182.09km/h (113.14mph).

Off the track and on the road, the fastest production road motorcycle in terms of top speed is claimed to be the 1,000cc Kawasaki Tu Atara YB6 E1. Generating 151bhp it flies along at up to 300km/h (186mph), well in excess of legal speeds, on this planet at least. The bike with the fastest acceleration is probably the brand new 120bhp Honda CBR 900RR Fireblade. It races from 0-96.5km/h (0-60mph) in less than 3 seconds, twice as fast as a Porsche.

Speed Stunts

Some riders are so skillful that they can make a motorbike go almost as fast on one wheel as on two. Riding a turbo-charged Suzuki 1100 at Bruntingthorpe Proving Ground, Leicestershire, England, on 3 July 1989, Steve Burns set a world record of 241km/h (150mph) for a wheelie.

Talking of stunt speed driving records, we mustn't leave the four-wheelers out of the reckoning. Sven-Erik Söderman,

Below: *The production motorcycle with the fastest acceleration in the world is possibly the Honda CBR 900RR.*

for example, has done amazing things with an Opel Kadette tipped up on two side wheels. Driving at Mora Siljan airport, Dalecarlia, Sweden, on 2 August 1990, he positively *sidled* along at an unofficial world record speed of 164.38km/h (102.14mph)!

Some Record Journeys

Most speed records have been achieved over fairly short distances, but some intrepid travelers have set out to cover whole tracts of the Earth — even the Earth itself — at the fastest possible speed.

The world circumnavigation record currently stands at 39 days 23 hours 35 minutes. It was achieved in May-June 1990 by a British team from the Royal Army Ordnance Corps driving two Rover 827Si saloons. Their start and finish point was the Tower of London. Since they covered a distance of 40,534.7km (25,187.8 miles), their average speed was 42.16km/h (26.2mph).

This was a little faster than that achieved by Garry Sowerby of Canada and Tim Cahill of the USA on their record-setting Trans-Americas drive in September-October 1987. Traveling in a GMC Sierra 4wd pick-up, they covered the 23,720km (14,739miles) from Tierra del Fuego to Prudhoe Bay, Alaska, USA, in a total of 23 days 22 hours 43 minutes, averaging 41.26km/h (25.64mph) for the whole journey.

John and Lucy Hemsley upped the average speed considerably on their epic Cape to London journey in January 1983. Using a Range Rover, they succeeded in covering the 18,787km (11,674miles) of road in just 14 days 19 hours 26 minutes, thus averaging 52.78km/h (32.8mph) — a remarkable speed considering that most of the journey was across Africa.

Railways

The one category of land vehicles capable of high speed movement which we have not yet looked at is railways.

Surprising though it may seem, there is one train in regular service on a national railway system which is capable of traveling at over 482.7km/h (300mph). This is the famous TGV (Train à Grande Vitesse), a French train which is both literally and metaphorically electric (actually gas turbine with electric transmission). In May 1990, while running from north to south

Below: *If you really want to take the fast train, then what you need to catch is the French Railways' TGV.*

between Courtalain and Tours, it notched up a world record speed of 515km/h (320mph). The TGV's main drawback is that it does not tilt at bends and therefore needs specially built straight track if it is to run at full speed.

At the time, however, it wasn't carrying any passengers. The speed record for a passenger-carrying train is held by the Japanese Maglev (Magnetic Levitation) test train MLU-001. On 4 February 1987, while running on a Japanese National Railway experimental track at Miyazaki, it reached a speed of 400.7km/h (249mph). The difference between a Maglev and a conventional train is that when in motion the Maglev does not actually touch the track, so reducing friction.

For a diesel train the speed record is 238.9km/h (148.4mph). This was achieved by a special British Rail train powered by two InterCity 125 diesel locomotives while testing coach bogies between Darlington and York. The run took place in November 1987.

The generally-acknowledged speed record for a steam train is held by another British loco — the famous LNER *Mallard*. Setting off from Barkston, north of Grantham in Lincolnshire on the east coast main line, on 3 July 1938, it hauled its 244-tonne train (including a special measuring coach) down the 12.9km (8mile) Stoke bank at a maximum speed of 210.16km/h (125mph), Driver Duddington at the controls. The great engine (which alone weighed 170 tons) was really straining though, for afterwards it was found to have sustained severe damage to its middle cylinder big end and crank pin — not surprising when its wheels were turning at 500 rpm.

Right: *A diesel HST.125, seen in 1985 two years before the record-breaking Darlington to York run.*

Left: *The LNER Class A4 loco No. 4468* Mallard, *which broke the speed record for a steam locomotive back in 1938.*

There are several stories of steam locos pulling trains at greater speeds than *Mallard*. A huge T1 of Pennsylvania Railroad, for example, was said to have taken a 16-car train of nearly 1,000 tonnes up to 209km/h (130mph) on the Chicago-Harrisburg main line in the 1940s. Unfortunately there is no acceptable evidence to support this claim, but the T1 was an exceptionally powerful engine weighing almost three times as much as *Mallard*, and it was probably capable of such a fantastic feat. This, however, must remain speculation since we do not know any more than this.

Elevators and Cablecars

Some elevators and escalators can attain surprisingly high speeds. In the 'Sunshine 60' building in Tokyo, Japan, for example, the elevators operate at speeds up to 36.56km/h (22.72mph). Built by Mitsubishi, they are the fastest domestic passenger elevators in the world.

Some winding shafts in mines are twice as fast as this. One in South Africa, for example, operates at speeds of up to 65.2km/h or 1,095metres per minute (40.9mph or 3,595ft per minute). It needs to, because its shaft is 2,072 metres (6,800ft) deep. It is doubtful whether there are any faster elevators than this.

The fastest cablecar in the world is believed to be the Teleférico Mérida in Venezuela. It has two cars, each of which holds 45 passengers, and they are hauled up to the summit of Pico Espejo (4,764metres-15,630ft) at a speed of 35.08km/h (21.8mph).

Section Two: Water

The Story of the Water Speed Record

Being displacement vessels dependent on the wind, sailing ships have always been limited in their ability to increase their speed. Even the early motorboats found it impossible to top the 64km/h (40mph) mark because they were displacement vessels too.

When planing bottom hulls which skimmed along the surface of the water came along, the water speed record began to rise in leaps and bounds. In 1914 it was 80.5km/h (50mph). By 1931 it had gone up to over 160km/h (100mph). And by 1955 it had doubled again, to over 321.9km/h (200mph).

Until relatively recently, the struggle to win the world water speed record was essentially a two-nation affair. Between 1928 and 1978 all the official holders were either British or American.

The greatest figures in the history of the water speed record are Sir Malcolm Campbell and his son Donald. Between them they broke the record no fewer than ten times between 1938 and 1964. Having retired from the land speed record, Sir Malcolm Campbell turned his attention to water and broke the record twice, the last time in 1939 with 228.04km/h (141.7mph).

After the American Stanley Sayers had raised it to 282.27km/h (178.5mph), Donald Campbell entered the lists with his jet-powered *Bluebird K7*. He broke through 321.8km/h

(200mph) in 1955, and thereafter set a further six records culminating in 444.66km/h (276.3mph) in 1964 — the year in which he became the first man to break both the land and water speed records in the same year.

Campbell was on course for an eighth record in 1967 when his boat somersaulted and disintegrated at over 482.7km/h (300mph), killing him instantly. Following Sir Henry Segrave in 1930 and John Cobb in 1952, Campbell thus became the third of Britain's LSR holders to lose his life on the vastly more volatile element of water.

The US held the record once more, with Lee Taylor's turbojet *Hustler*, before it passed to the Australians.

Powered Craft

The fastest machine on water is Australian Kenneth Warby's hydroplane *Spirit of Australia*. On 8 October 1978 he set the world water speed record on Blowering Dam Lake, New South Wales, Australia, by driving his boat at 514.389km/h (319.64mph). Warby's unofficial best speed was actually considerably higher than that. In November of the previous year, on the same lake, he had touched an estimated 556km/h (345.49mph). For the moment that is generally accepted as the fastest anyone has ever been on water.

The next fastest boats are 150km/h (93.2mph) or more slower. These are propeller-driven drag boats, the champion of which is *The Texan*, a Kurtis Top Fuel Hydro Drag Boat. Driven by Eddie Kramer at Chowchilla, California, USA, on

5 September 1982, this boat attained the remarkable speed of 368.52km/h (229mph). Three years later, a similar hydroboat *Final Effort*, driven by Robert Burns at Creve Coeur Lake, St Louis, Missouri, USA, touched a slightly slower speed of 360.29km/h (223.88mph). For technical reasons this is the one recognized by the American Drag Boat Association.

Below: *Carlo Bonomi; in 1985 driver of the world's fastest diesel-powered boat,* Iveco World Leader.

According to the Union Internationale Motonautique, the fastest speed for an outboard-powered vessel is 285.83km/h (177.61mph). P R Knight, driving a Chevrolet-powered Lautobach, hit this speed on Lake Ruataniwha, New Zealand, in 1986. In the same year Robert Hering set the world Formula One record of 266.085km/h (165.338mph) at Parker, Arizona, USA.

Dropping down the scale a little, the fastest offshore boats are capable of around 245km/h (152.2mph). The actual record of 248.537km/h (154.438mph) is held by Tom Gentry of the USA, who in March 1987 drove a 15metre (49ft) catamaran powered by four turbo-charged V8 engines.

The fastest diesel boat is the Aifo-Fiat powered hydroplane *Iveco World Leader*. Driven by Carlo Bonomi at Venice, Italy, in April 1985, it reached a speed of 218.248km/h (135.532mph).

The record for an electrically-powered powerboat is well under half that. Standing at 83.64km/h (51.973mph), it was set by 71-year-old countess, Fiona, Lady Arran, driving her 4.57metre (15ft) hydroplane *Strandag* (Gaelic for 'Spark') at Holme Pierrepoint, UK, in November 1989.

Hovercraft

Besides powerboats — boats built specifically for speed — other fast water-going vessels include hovercraft. Although some can also skim over land, they are normally associated with aquatic travel.

The fastest hovercraft in the world is the US Navy test vehicle SES-100 B built by Bell Aerosystems. Pedestrian its name may be, but its performance certainly isn't. Out on the Chesapeake Bay Test Range, Maryland, USA, in January 1980 it reached 91.9knots (170km/h-105.8mph).

Above: *The US Navy's record-breaking Bell SES-100B hovercraft on a test run off the Florida coast in 1976.*

Because of their speed, hovercraft were soon introduced into the cross-channel service between England and France. In September 1984 an SRN 4 Mark II Mountbatten class completed the 40km (25mile) Dover-Calais run in a record time of 24 minutes 8.4 seconds, thus averaging about 96km/h (60mph). The previous record of 52 minutes 49 seconds had been held by a conventional ferry, Townsend Thoresen's *Spirit of Free Enterprise*.

If we disregard the hovercraft, the fastest boat across the English Channel, and probably the world's fastest passenger ferry, is Hoverspeed's catamaran passenger ferry known familiarly as the SeaCat. On 15 October 1991 Hoverspeed *France* set a new record for the Dover-Calais run of 34 minutes 23 seconds, meaning an average speed of nearly 72km/h (45mph). Not much slower than the hovercraft, the SeaCat can nevertheless carry over 100 more passengers (383) and more than double the number of cars (80).

If we disregard the SeaCat as well as the hovercraft, the fastest conventional car and passenger ferry in the world is the 24,065grt (gross registered tonnage) Finnjet. Operating between Helsinki, Finland, and Travemunde, Germany, it is quite capable of steaming in excess of 30knots (55.5km/h-34mph).

Among hydrofoils (craft with sea wings designed to lift their hulls out of the water and thus reduce drag), the fastest ever was a Boeing research hydrofoil named *FRESH-1* (Foil Research Supercavitating Hydrofoil 1). Powered by an aircraft turbofan engine, it was capable of 105knots (194.6km/h-120.9mph).

The fastest regular hydrofoil was *Plainview*, built for the US Navy by the Lockheed Shipbuilding and Construction Co at Seattle, Washington State, USA, in 1965. Weighing 314 tonnes with a full load, and also the largest hydrofoil in the world, it had been designed for a top speed of 80knots (148km/h-92mph), but was in practice capable of no more than 50knots (92.5km/h-57.5mph).

Military Craft

Besides being the fastest hovercraft the US Navy test machine SES-100B is also the world's fastest warship.

The fastest cruiser of all time was probably Italy's *Alberto di Giussano*, first of a class of 6,000 ton vessels with 95,000hp steam turbine engines. At her trials in 1931 she reached 42.05 knots (77.9km/h-48.42mph). During World War II one of her sister ships was caught and sunk by an Allied warship, so perhaps in practice they were not so fast after all.

The fastest destroyer ever was the French ship of the Le Fantasque class, *Le Terrible*, launched as long ago as 1935. Built at Blainville in France, weighing 2,830 tonnes, and powered by two turbines generating 100,000shp, it could sail at over 45 knots (83.4km/h-51.5mph). 46.25 knots (83.42km/h/ 52.10mph) was actually the speed recorded at her acceptance trials in 1935.

The fastest submarine is thought to be the Russian Alfa class of nuclear-powered vessels. With a weight of 2,700 tons (surface) and 3,600 tons (submerged), they are said to be capable of 45 knots (83.4km/h-51.5mph). This is despite the fact that the oldest of them — laid down in the mid-sixties and completed in 1970 — is now over 20 years old.

In the absence of precise figures, the US Navy's Los Angeles class is also a serious contender for the mantle of fastest sub. The submerged speed is classified, but guesstimates put it at over 40 knots (74km/h/46mph). Each one cost about $220 million (£114 million) at mid 1970s' prices.

Fastest of all displacement warships were the high-speed motorboats popular in World War II and later. The fastest ever

Below: *The destroyer* Le Fantasque *of the Le Fantasque class — sister ship to* Le Terrible — *seen here in 1936.*

Above: *The CIS Alfa class nuclear submarine. Its high speed was designed to elude NATO torpedoes.* **Below:** *The USS* Honolulu *of the Los Angeles class. The hull is specially built for high submerged speeds.*

Above: *The Vosper MTB 102, the fastest piston-engined boat, seen here during trials in the Solent in 1938.*

were the British Royal Navy's Brave class, built in the 1950s by Vosper. Powered by 4 Proteus gas turbine engines (the same as used in the Britannia airliner), they were capable of 52knots-plus (96.37km/h-60mph).

The British motor torpedo boat MTB 102 of 1937, also built by Vosper, was the fastest of the traditional piston-engined motorboats. It could reach a top speed of 47.8knots (88.4km/h-54.9mph).

Above: *The* Gentry Eagle *at speed in the Atlantic, with (inset) its builder, American millionaire Tom Gentry.*

Record Journey Times

American millionaire Tom Gentry set the record for the fastest crossing of the Atlantic by boat in July 1989 when his 33.5 metre (109.94ft) *Gentry Eagle* reached Bishop Rock Lighthouse off the English coast, having started from Ambrose Light Tower, in 62 hours 7 minutes 47 seconds. His speed made good was 45.7knots (84.5km/h-52.5mph).

Being a boat bred for speed with no pretensions to commercial use, *Gentry Eagle* did not qualify for the Blue Riband,

symbolized by the Hales Trophy, which is awarded to the fastest passenger ship across the Atlantic.

For many years this was held by the *United States*, a 52,000-ton high-speed liner which made its record-breaking run on its maiden voyage out of New York in 1952. Setting off on 3 July, she reached Bishop Rock Lighthouse 3 days

34

10 hours 40 minutes later, having averaged an amazing 35.59knots (66km/h-41mph). The highest speed she ever attained, during sea trials in June 1952, was 38.32knots (71.01km/h-44.12mph).

In the 1980s Richard Branson, head of the Virgin company, revived interest in the Blue Riband/Hales Trophy by his

Below: *Briton Richard Branson (inset) also tried for the transatlantic record in his boat* Virgin Atlantic.

transatlantic record attempts designed to generate publicity for his new airline. He did set a new record, but he did not win the trophy because his boat, like Gentry's, was not destined for commercial use.

The current holder of the Hales Trophy is *Hoverspeed Great Britain*, one of the Hoverspeed SeaCats in service on the cross-channel ferry route between England and France. In June 1990, two months before it entered service, *Great Britain* crossed the Atlantic from the Nantucket Light Buoy to

Bishop Rock Lighthouse in 79 hours 15 minutes, averaging 36.966knots (68.3km/h-42.4mph), only 1.5knots faster than the much bigger *United States*. But it was only with extreme reluctance that the American Merchant Maritime Museum surrendered the Hales Trophy, for they claimed that the SeaCat was hardly a passenger liner in the sense that the *United States* was. They did of course have a point, but the SeaCat is undoubtedly a commercial passenger ship, which is more than can be said for the next two likely contenders for the trophy.

One is the *Spirit of Newcastle*, a futuristically-designed boat powered by an engine from a Lockheed Tristar and funded by companies and individuals in the northeast of England. The other is *Destriero* (meaning 'steed' or 'war-horse'), an Italian boat backed by a shadowy consortium of big businessmen. Powered by no fewer than three General Electric aero engines (the US FA-18 Hornet jet fighter makes do with two), the *Destriero* can attain speeds in excess of 59knots (112km/h-70mph) despite its 400-ton weight.

One of these two will almost certainly set a new transatlantic crossing record, but it is hard to see how either will successfully claim commercial status and thus secure the Blue Riband Hales Trophy.

The Pacific does not hold the same attraction for speed merchants as the Atlantic, no doubt for perfectly good reasons. The result is that the record for crossing that shark-infested expanse of ocean (could the sharks be one of the reasons?) is held not by some high-tech powerboat or new-generation

Right: *The current holder of the Hales Trophy for the transatlantic run is* Hoverspeed Great Britain.

36

high-speed passenger ferry, but by a plain old merchant vessel, namely the *Sea-Land Commerce* container ship. Setting off from Yokohama, Japan, on 30 June 1973, it arrived at Long Beach, California, USA, 6 days 1 hour 27 minutes later. The 50,315-ton ship averaged 33.27knots (61.65km/h-38.2mph) on its voyage.

Finally in this section, the speed record for an offshore race currently stands at 166.22km/h (103.29mph). It was set by Tony Garcia of the US in a Class 1 powerboat at Key West, Florida, USA, in November 1983.

Wind-Powered Vessels

The highest speeds attained by wind-powered vessels on water are inevitably much lower than those reached by powered craft. Nevertheless the record for any sailing vessel (over a 500metre timed run) is a very respectable 44.66knots (82.71km/h-51.3mph). The vessel in question was a sailboard (windsurfer), and was sailed by Frenchman Thierry Bielak at Saintes Maries-de-la-Mer, Camargue, southern France, on 18 April 1991.

Bielak was able to achieve such a high speed because he was sailing on the calm sheltered canal at Saintes Maries. Sailboarding on the sea inevitably reduces speed slightly, so that the equivalent *marine* as opposed to *water* record is 42.91knots (79.3km/h-49.2mph). This speed (actually average for the 500 metre timed run) was achieved by another Frenchman, Pascal Maka, offshore at Saintes Maries de-la-Mer in February 1990.

Left: *The Hales Trophy. Also known as the 'Blue Riband', it is awarded to the fastest commercial liner across the Atlantic.*

The fastest sailing boat over 500metres is Russell Long's *Longshot*, a 6.3 metre (20ft 9in) trifoiler. Sailing it at Lethbridge, Canada, on 12 October 1990, he covered the distance in 26.17 seconds, thus averaging 37.14knots (68.7km/-42.6mph). Of course, to produce this average speed, his top speed must have been a little faster.

The record for the full nautical mile (1.85km-1.14 miles) is held by the 22.6 metre (74ft) catamaran *Crédit Agricole (II)*. Skippered by Frenchman Philippe Jeantot, it completed its short course in just 2 minutes 13 seconds (27.1knots smg).

Some of the old clipper ships achieved remarkable speeds in their day and one still holds the record for the longest day's run under sail for any sailing vessel. Running before a north-westerly gale in the southern Indian Ocean in December 1854, the appropriately-named *Champion of the Seas* of the Liverpool Black Ball Line covered 461.5 nautical miles (nm) in a little under 24 hours, thus averaging 19.8knots (36.63km/h-22.7mph). Or so it is claimed. Some experts dispute the figure as impossible, and say the real record is the 370nm (684.5km-425 miles) in the south Pacific achieved by the five-masted barque *Preussen* under Captain Petersen. But even this record has its doubters. What seems beyond contradiction, however, is *Preussen's* record for the highest speed measured over a four-hour watch: 17.5knots (32.4km/h-20.15mph).

Another Liverpool ship, the *James Baines*, accomplished the fastest circumnavigation by a clipper when it sailed out to Melbourne, Australia, and back in just 133 days in 1854-55 (a further 28 days were spent in port). This compares favourably with an absolute record for a circumnavigation under sail (west to east, non-stop) of 109 days 8 hours 48 minutes 50 seconds achieved by the 18.3 metre (60ft) cutter *Ecureuil d'Aquitaine II* in the Vendée Globe Challenge Race between November 1989 and March 1990. The skipper was Frenchman Titouan Lamazou.

Moving on to other record journey times, the fastest crossing of the Atlantic by a sailing boat was achieved in June 1990,

Below: Jet Services 5, *the catamaran which is current holder of the fastest transatlantic trip by sail.*

when the *Jet Services 5* catamaran sloop crossed west-to-east from Ambrose Light Tower to Lizard Lighthouse in only 6 days 13 hours 3 minutes 32 seconds (18.4knots smg). The east-west record of 10 days 23 hours 15 minutes (11knots smg: east-west is always slower because the prevailing winds blow from the west) was set in the same month by the 18.3 metre (60ft) trimaran sloop *Elf Aquitaine III*, sailing from Plymouth to Newport, Rhode Island. Both boats were skippered by Frenchmen — Serge Madec and Jean Maurel respectively. (The old clipper ship records were 12 days west-east and 15 days east-west.)

Below: Elf Aquitaine III *leading the way and breaking speed records in the two-handed transatlantic race, 1990.*

Above: *In choppy seas, the American sloop* Nirvana *races ahead during its record-breaking Fastnet run of 1985.*

Record Race Times

The two premier ocean sailing races are the Newport, Rhode Island-Bermuda (American), and the Fastnet (British). The course of the American race measures 635nm (1,176km-730.2 miles) and the record for it is 2 days 14 hours 29 minutes (average speed 10.16knots-18.81km/h-11.6mph). The course of the British race is slightly shorter — 605nm (1,123km-697.3 miles) — and its record completion time is 2 days 12 hours 41 minutes (average speed 9.97knots-18.45km/h-11.5mph). Both records were set by the American sloop *Nirvana*, in 1982 and 1985 respectively.

Section Three: Air and Space

The Story of the Air Speed Record

Although the first men to fly were Americans, it was the French who dominated aviation's early years. Louis Blériot took the speed prize with 76.95km/h (47.8mph) at the world's first international aviation meeting held at Rheims, France, in 1909.

By the time World War I broke out the record stood at 203.81km/h (126.64mph).

The 321.8km/h (200mph) barrier was broken when the great French racer Sadi Lecointe averaged 329.6km/h (206mph) in 1925.

The Italians topped 482.7km/h (300mph) in 1928 and then the British cracked 643.7km/h (400mph) in 1931 with a Supermarine S6B Schneider Trophy-winning seaplane flown by an RAF pilot. Developed and flown under government sponsorship, the Schneider seaplane competitors were the fastest planes of all in the late '20s and early '30s.

The air speed record returned to landplanes in 1939 when the Germans pushed it to well over 724.1km/h (450mph) on two successive occasions. The second — 755.14km/h (469.22mph) by Fritz Wendel at Augsburg in April 1939 — remained the piston-engined speed record for an amazing 30 years. Darryl Greenmayer of the US eventually broke this speed barrier in 1969 in a modified Grumman F8F Bearcat of World War II vintage.

Left: *A rocket-powered Bell X-1 research aircraft. It was a similar plane that first broke the sound barrier.*

Above: *Captain 'Chuck' Yeager at the controls of the X-1 — together they caused the first sonic boom.*

Meanwhile, the new jet aircraft developed during the war had opened up the possibility of incredible new air speed records. Chuck Yeager broke the speed of sound in 1947 in a Bell X-1 research aircraft. A Bell X-2 topped Mach 3 in 1956.

Being air-launched, the Bell X-craft records were not official. The official record stayed with more conventional aircraft, such as the British Fairey Delta 2, which exceeded 1,609.2km/h (1,000mph) in 1956. By 1961 US Phantoms and Russian MiGs were flying at new world record speeds.

Jet-Powered Aircraft

The fastest aircraft ever made was the US development plane codenamed the X-15. At the limit of the X-15 research program (it never went into production), NASA civilian pilot William Knight flew an X-15A-2 on 3 October 1967 at 7,297km/h (4,534mph-Mach 6.72), in the process setting an unofficial world air speed record. It could not be official because the X-15 had to be launched from the air. Only NASA's shuttle orbiter — half aeroplane, half spacecraft — can beat the X-15 on speed. We look more closely at the shuttle later in the 'space' part of this section.

Above: *NASA's air-launched X-15 rocket-plane. It broke records and helped develop NASA's shuttle orbiter.*
Right: *The X-15 at the moment of launch. Its speed records were unofficial because it was air-launched.*

The official air speed record was set in July 1976, when Captain Eldon Joersz and Major George Morgan of the US Air Force flew at 3,529.56km/h (2,193.167mph) over Beale Air Force Base, California, USA.

Not surprisingly, the plane they flew on their record-breaking run — a Lockheed SR-71, nicknamed 'Blackbird' because

of its special heat-radiating, radar-absorbing black paint —
is also the world's fastest jet. Powered by two Pratt & Whitney
turbojets, this two-seat reconnaissance aircraft is reportedly
capable of flying at 3,620km/h (2,250mph).

The first SR-71s were ordered at the end of 1962. SR stands
for 'Strike/Reconnaissance'. The designation should actually
have been RS but President Lyndon Johnson inadvertently
transposed the initials when announcing the program at a
press conference. Only a few were built, despite the fact that
they proved to be extremely reliable and effective. No other
plane has held the air speed record for longer, and the actual
one used by Joersz and Morgan to set the record had already
done ten years' operational flying. In 1989 the planes were
taken out of service for financial reasons. There are no
successors.

Not much slower than the SR-71, the CIS Mikoyan MiG-25
(codenamed 'Foxbat' by NATO) is capable of Mach 3.2 or
3,395km/h (2,110mph) in its reconnaissance mode — 'Foxbat-
B'. We know this because in 1973 one was tracked by radar
at this speed while flying over Israel. In its normal mode as
an interceptor armed with air-to-air missiles, it is a little slower:
Mach 2.8 or 2,969km/h (1,845mph) is then the single-seat
Foxbat's maximum operating speed. This is still enough,
however, to make it the world's fastest combat jet. Powered
by twin-Tumanskii R-32 turbojets, the MiG-25 was developed
in the 1960s to counter the potential threat from the North
American XB-70 high altitude Mach 3 bomber. Production
of the MiG-25 ceased in the mid-1980s.

Left: *The Lockheed SR-71's two big turbojet engines generate
14,742kg (32,500lb) of thrust each.*

Above: *The SR-71 travels so high and so fast that the two-man
crew have to dress like astronauts.*

As well as being one of the largest, heaviest and most powerful aircraft ever built, the XB-70, called the 'Valkyrie', was also the fastest bomber ever. On 19 May 1966 one cruised at Mach 3 for 33 minutes over the western US, at one point reaching Mach 3.08 (3,277km/h-2,036mph). Despite its literally superlative attributes, the 'Valkyrie' never went into production — perhaps because of its equally superlative cost. Each flight swallowed up $800,000 (£416,000)!

Today the speed position with bombers is not quite clear. It would appear that the US General Dynamics swing-wing FB-111A, which has a top speed of Mach 2.5, is the fastest, although the CIS swing-wing Tupolev Tu-22M could be a match for it: it has an estimated over-target speed of Mach 2.0 and

Below: *The North American XB-70 'Valkyrie' on a research flight in 1968. Only two of these planes were built.*

Above: *The Tu-22M 'Backfire' strategic attack aircraft of the CIS was first developed in the late 1960s.*

Below: *The Dassault Mirage IV; an attack bomber whose speed compares favorably with the Tu-22M and FB-111A.*

could possibly do Mach 2.5. What is certain is that the French Dassault Mirage IV can fly at Mach 2.2 or 2,233.3km/h (1,450mph) at 11,000metres (36,000ft). Pending official confirmation of the US and CIS speeds, the Mirage would seem to be entitled to be called the world's fastest operational bomber.

The fastest V/STOL (Vertical/Short Take Off-Landing) aircraft is probably the brand-new CIS Yakovlev Yak-141, a single-seat carrier-based air combat fighter/attack aircraft officially unveiled at the 1991 Paris Air Show. Claims on behalf of this aircraft for twelve international records have already been submitted to the FAI, and a speed record attempt over a closed circuit is planned. At present the Yak is believed to be capable of 1,800km/h (1,118.5mph).

Speed Records

Moving away from the military theatre, the fastest civilian SST (supersonic transport) used to be the USSR's Tupolev Tu-144, which had a maximum cruising speed of 2,500km/h (1,550mph-Mach 2.35). Now out of service, its place has been taken by the famous droop-nosed supersonic jet Concorde, which can cruise at up to Mach 2.2 or 2,333km/h (1,450mph) but normally stays at Mach 2.05 to conserve fuel and prolong airframe life.

Developed by BAC in Britain and Aérospatiale in France, it has been in service with Air France and British Airways since January 1976 and carries up to 100 passengers. Its fastest time for the New York-London run, set on 14 April 1990, is 2 hours 55 minutes 15 seconds.

Below: *Before being taken out of service, the fastest civilian supersonic transport used to be the Tupolev Tu-144.*

First flown nearly a quarter of a century ago, Concorde is now getting just a bit long in the tooth. In May 1990 five companies in Britain, France, Germany and the US set up a joint study group to develop a successor aircraft. The main innovation will be doubled seating capacity, but speed will also be increased slightly, perhaps to Mach 2.4. The Russians are also developing a new, medium-sized, long-range supersonic transport designated the Sukhoi S-51, but it is not yet clear just how fast this will go. Preliminary estimates, however, suggest that its maximum speed will probably be only Mach 2 or 1,000km/h (1,320mph) — in other words, slightly less than the current Concordes.

Above: *Now that accolade has gone to the Concorde, though its age may start to tell on its supersonic performance.*

Below: *A future replacement to Concorde could be the ATSF, capable of carrying 200 people at up to Mach 2.*

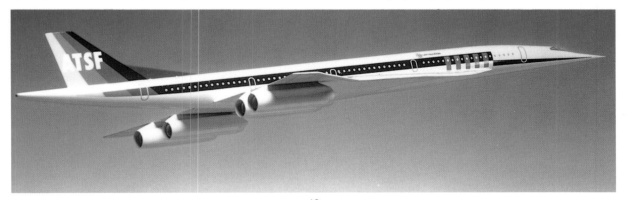

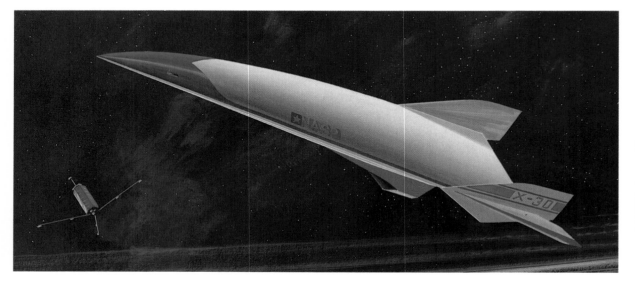

In the not too distant future, even second-generation Concorde times will seem slow, if the US National Aero-Space Plane (NASP) project gets off the ground. Jointly sponsored by the US Air Force and NASA, the NASP X-30 will take off and land on normal runways, cruise in the upper atmosphere at Mach 5-15 or 5,250-15,750km/h (3,000-10,000mph), and cut Tokyo-Washington flight times to two hours. The first one is expected to fly in the late 1990s.

Above: *The NASP project is scheduled to fly its X-30 experimental vehicle into Earth orbit by 1996.*

Other countries, including Britain with its HOTOL (Horizontal Take Off and Landing), have similar aerospace-plane projects. They have seen enormous commercial possibilities of such ultra-fast flights. None, however, is as far advanced or as likely to get off the ground as the American X-30.

Propeller-Driven Aircraft

Propeller-driven aircraft can fly at hundreds of miles an hour, but they have yet to break the Mach 1 barrier.

The turboprops are the fastest propeller-driven aircraft. The fastest of these would appear to be a McDonnell Douglas MD-80 prototype which flew at Mach 0.865 (912km/h-570mph) during tests in 1987-88.

But the fastest turboprop in current service is the CIS Tu-114, a four-engined transport developed from the Tupolev Tu-95 bomber which flew at 877.212km/h (545.076mph) with a heavy payload on board back in April 1960. This is in fact the highest ratified speed for any non-jet aircraft over any distance or with any load.

The official FAI speed record for a piston-engined aircraft was set in August 1989 when Lyle Shelton, a former US Navy and later TWA pilot, flew his Grumman F8F-2 *Rare Bear* at an average of 850.263km/h (528.35mph) over the requisite four runs near Las Vegas, New Mexico. Shelton originally bought the aircraft as an engineless wreck in 1968.

Shelton also holds the world time-to-height record for a propeller-driven aircraft. In February 1972, flying the same Grumman, he climbed from ground level to 3,000metres (9,842.5ft) in 91.92 seconds.

The biplane speed record is 520km/h (323mph). It was set by two aircraft within the space of three years. The first to achieve it, in December 1938, was the Canadian CCF Gregor FDB-1. The second was the Fiat CR 42DB, an Italian plane powered by a Daimler-Benz engine and flown in March 1941.

Left: *The revolutionary engine of the British HOTOL would be both airbreathing jet and oxygen/hydrogen rocket.*

Flying Boats and Floatplanes

The CIS Beriev M-10 holds the official flying boat record of 912km/h (566.69mph). It was set by Nikolay Andreyevskiy and his crew of two over a measured course on 7 August 1961.

As is often the case, however, there is a slightly higher but unofficial speed record for a flying boat, and this time it is held by an American plane, the Martin XP6M-1 Seamaster. Flown in the late '50s, this US Navy minelayer, powered by four jet engines, had a top speed of 1,400km/h (646mph). It was probably the fastest flying boat ever built.

The fastest of all the old Schneider Trophy floatplanes, so famous between the wars, was the Italian Macchi-Castoldi MC 72. Piloted by Francesco Agello, one reached 705km/h (440.68mph) in October 1934.

Helicopters and Other Aircraft

The fastest helicopters ever were two American research machines built in the 1960s. The Lockheed XH-51A, assisted by a J60 booster turbojet, achieved 487km/h (302.6mph) in June 1967. Two years later, a Bell 533 with *two* J60s achieved 509km/h (316mph).

Production helicopters have yet to crack the 402.3km/h (250mph) barrier. The world record at the moment is 400.87km/h (240.09mph), set by a British Westland Lynx flying over the Somerset levels in August 1986. The company itself was responsible for the record attempt. It used its own

Below: *The Lockheed XH-51A 'compound rotorcraft' in flight. Note the short wings and large turbine engine.*

chief test pilot (Trevor Eggington) and demonstration helicopter, and it treated the whole business as a serious technical exercise. The speed achieved was actually forecast in advance to within 1km/h (0.62mph).

The speed record for autogyros, which are like mini-helicopters, is about half that. It stands at 193.9km/h (120.5mph)

Above: *The Lynx during its successful world speed record attempt over southern England in August 1986.*

and it was set in Britain by Wing Commander Kenneth Wallis, managing director of Norfolk-based Wallis Autogyros Ltd, on 18 September 1986.

The speed record for airships was set by the giant British R100 when it flew at 131.2km/h (81.5mph) in January 1930. The R100, built in 1929, was scrapped the following year after its sister ship, the R101, had crashed, killing 46 people.

All these aircraft are, or were, capable of carrying humans. One must not forget though that comparatively small model aircraft can also achieve remarkably high speeds. Take the radio-controlled model plane belonging to V. Goukoune and V. Myakinin of the then USSR for example. On 21 September 1971 this little plane flew at 343.92km/h (213.7mph) over Klementyevo and set a world record in the process.

Record Journey Times

The FAI recognizes circumnavigations which exceed the length of the Tropics of Cancer or Capricorn (36,787.599km-22,858.754 miles) but which may not be as long as a full circumnavigation passing through two antipodal points (40,007.89km-24,859.75 miles). The fastest non-antipodal circumnavigation was made in January 1988 by a Boeing 747 carrying 141 passengers. Flying eastwards from Seattle,

Below: *The British R100 held the fastest airship record, but was scrapped in 1930 because of safety fears.*

Above: *The MiG-25 high-altitude interceptor of the CIS holds the record for the fastest time to height record.*

Washington State, USA, it completed its circular trip in 36 hours 54 minutes 15 seconds, covering 37,216km (23,125 miles) in the process, and stopping only twice to refuel. Its average speed was about 1,005.79km/h (625mph).

The average speed of the aircraft which made the fastest ever crossing of the Atlantic was, amazingly, three times that. Speeding the 5,570.80nm (5,538.5km-3,461.53 miles) between New York and London in just 1 hour 54 minutes 56.4 seconds in September 1974, the Lockheed SR-71A (also the fastest jet in the world — see above, page 45) piloted by Major James Sullivan and Major Noel Widdifield averaged an incredible 2,9087.026km/h (1,806.963mph). Had the aircraft not had to slow down for mid-air refueling, its average speed would have been even higher.

Some planes can also fly phenomenally fast in a vertical direction. The record here — the fastest time-to-height record — is held by the world's fastest combat jet (see above, page 45), the MiG-25. A MiG flown by Aleksandr Fedotov of the then USSR on 17 May 1975 reached a height of 30,000 metres (98,425ft) — in other words the fringe of space — just 4 minutes 11.4 seconds after take-off.

Free-Flight Aircraft

The *Virgin Otsuka Pacific Flyer* crewed by Richard Branson and Per Lindstrand appears to hold the world speed record for a hot-air balloon. When it made the first ever crossing of the Pacific by a craft of its kind in January 1991 it maintained 385km/h (239mph) for one hour during the flight. Of course, in truth balloons cannot really have airspeeds (speed relative to the surrounding atmosphere) because the wind is their motive force. On the other hand, because they are driven by the wind they can reach considerable ground speeds.

The speed record for a glider (over a 100 metre-109.4 yards triangular course) is 195.3km/h (121.35mph). It was set by Ingo Renner of Australia flying a Nimbus 3 on 14 December 1982. Had Pete Di Giacomo's kite been up there at the time there could have been quite a tussle for first place, for the American's kite flew at 193km/h (120mph) at Ocean City, Maryland, USA, on 22 September 1989.

Below: *The crew of the* Virgin Otsuka Pacific Flyer, *Per Lindstrand and entrepreneur/adventurer Richard Branson.*

Above: *The dramatic sight of the* Virgin Otsuka Pacific Flyer, *prior to take-off.*

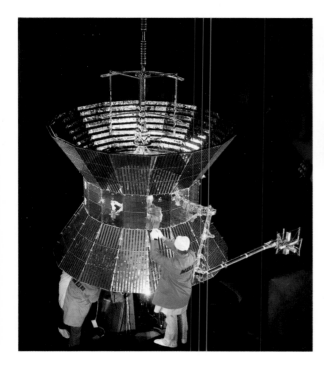

Above: *The crew of the Apollo 10 spacecraft during the second manned orbital flight of the Moon, May 1969.*

Space

Out in gravity-less space, speeds inevitably far exceed those achieved on Earth. You have, in any case, to achieve a very high velocity to break out of the Earth's atmosphere.

The fastest-recorded machine in space is the NASA-German Helios B solar probe, despatched on its long mission on 15 January 1976. Every time it reaches the perihelion of its solar orbit it touches 252,800km/h (158,000mph). Compared with this incredible velocity, the human speed record in space seems positively modest at 39,897km/h (24,791mph). It was set in May 1969 when Colonel Thomas Stafford, Commander Eugene Cernan and Commander John Young were riding in the Apollo 10 command module on its journey back to Earth. Their altitude at the time was 121.9km (400,000ft).

Above: *The NASA-German solar probe Helios B was designed to measure energy and cosmic dust around the Sun.*

Above: *The Apollo 16 Rover, the fastest Lunar Rover on the Moon, seen here with a crew member, 22 April 1972.*

(Since we are in space it may be the right time to mention that the 'land' speed record on the Moon is the 18km/h (11.2mph) achieved by the unmanned Apollo 16 Rover. It was traveling downhill at the time!)

The US shuttle *Columbia*, launched from the Kennedy Space Center, Cape Canaveral, in April 1981 is the world's fastest fixed-wing aircraft, but since it is really designed for

Left: *Like an aircraft, the NASA shuttle orbiter* Columbia *touches down on Earth after a successful trip into space.*

space travel we have included it in this section. When its main engine ceased burning, it was traveling at 26,715km/h (16,000mph). *Endeavour*, the $26 billion (£13 billion) shuttle ordered by NASA in 1987 as a replacement for the crashed orbiter *Challenger* is probably going to be a bit faster. Its intended orbital speed is 28,325km/h (17,600mph). The shuttle *Endeavour* first flew in May 1992.

Section Four: Weapons, Machines & Apparatus

Weapons

The speed of weapons can be measured in two ways: the speed of the projectile, be it arrow, bullet, shell or missile; and the rate at which the projectiles are dispatched over a given period of time. Where appropriate, the speed of the projectile is referred to as muzzle velocity, or mv.

The record for a flight arrow fired by a modern longbow is 152 metres a second (499ft a second-547.5km/h-340.2mph). An arrow from a medieval longbow would probably have flown at less than half that speed: 64.1metres per second (143.5mph) is one modern estimate.

The highest muzzle velocity (mv) for small arms is 1,410metres per second (9,150ft per second) reached by a 1lb fin-stabilized projectile fired by a Canadian Armament Research and Development Establishment gun. The mv of a typical modern tank or anti-tank gun is roughly 1,463metres per second (4,800ft per second).

The fastest missiles must be the great ICBMs (Intercontinental Ballistic Missiles) produced in such large numbers since World War II. These must attain speeds approaching 27,400km/h (17,000mph) in order to be able to break out of the Earth's atmosphere and maintain their trajectory. From their high point some 966km (600 miles) above the Earth they would free-fall down onto their target.

Left: *The test launch of the MX type ICBM in 1983; possibly the fastest and most destructive of weapons.*

Above: *Launching the MK 48 torpedo from the deck of a US Navy ship. It is being replaced by the even faster MK 60.*

The speediest torpedo is believed to be the American MK 48. This is capable of about 50 knots (93km/h-57.8mph), twice the speed of a standard torpedo.

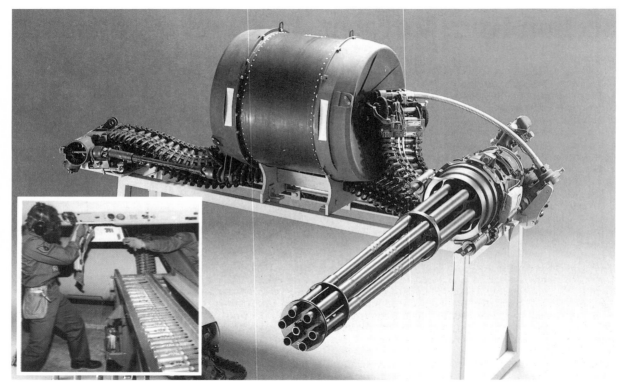

Above: *The McDonnell Douglas F-1E Strike Eagle, one of the latest fighters to carry the Vulcan gun.*

The gun with the highest rate of fire is probably the American M61A-2 Vulcan, a Gatling-type machinegun with six barrels each of which fires in turn. At its standard 20mm caliber, it fires 6,000 rounds per minute or 100 rounds a second. But at 5.56mm, the rate increases to 10,000 shots per minute.

Machines and Apparatus
The fastest speed ever achieved by a continuously rotating Earthbound object is 7,250km/h (4,500mph). The object in question was a 15.2 cm (6in) carbon fiber rod turning in a vacuum at Birmingham University, England, in January 1975. The rod was set in a hub and supported by the field of an electron magnet so that it touched no other solid object.

Left: *The awesome-looking M61A-2 Vulcan multi-barreled gun, and (inset) loading the gun inside an aircraft.*

In complete contrast, the slowest machine on Earth appears to be a nuclear environmental machine for testing stress corrosion. Developed by Nene Instruments of Wellingborough, Northants, England, it can be slowed right down until it is moving at a speed of only 1 million millionth of a millimetre per minute, or 1cm (0.394in) in every 20 million years.

In October 1968, Illinois State University in the USA announced the development of a transistor capable of switching 230,000 million times a second. It is thought to be the fastest in the world (one cannot imagine how it could be otherwise).

The world's fastest (as well as most powerful) computer is the liquid-cooled CRAY-2, developed by computer genius Seymour Cray's Cray Research Inc of Minneapolis, Minnesota, USA. It can carry out 250 million floating point operations per second and it has 32 million bytes of main memory.

Of all production cameras, the fastest is the Imacon 675 cine camera made by Hadland Photonics Ltd, Herts, England, Its 600 million frames per second, however, is nothing compared with a special research camera built at the Imperial College of Science and Technology in London. This can register images at the rate of 33 billion frames per second. Ordinary cine cameras operate at 30 frames per second.

When it comes to printing, you cannot find anything faster than the electro-sensitive system at the Lawrence Radiation Laboratory, Livermore, California, USA. Making use of electronic pulses, chemically-impregnated paper and multiple styluses, it can churn out printed material of Bible length in just over 1 minute (65 seconds for 773,692 words to be precise).

Index

Entries in *italics* refer to illustrations